Parenting Toddlers

How to Handle Different Parenting Styles in Your Family and Become a Fantastic Parent

(Positive Parenting and Everyday Solutions to Parenting Problems)

Steven Junkins

Published by Rob Miles

© **Steven Junkins**

All Rights Reserved

Parenting Toddlers: How to Handle Different Parenting Styles in Your Family and Become a Fantastic Parent (Positive Parenting and Everyday Solutions to Parenting Problems)

ISBN 978-1-990084-23-2

All rights reserved. No part of this guide may be reproduced in any form without permission in writing from the publisher except in the case of brief quotations embodied in critical articles or reviews.

Legal & Disclaimer

The information contained in this book is not designed to replace or take the place of any form of medicine or professional medical advice. The information in this book has been provided for educational and entertainment purposes only.

The information contained in this book has been compiled from sources deemed reliable, and it is accurate to the best of the Author's knowledge; however, the Author cannot guarantee its accuracy and validity and cannot be held liable for any errors or omissions. Changes are periodically made to this book. You must consult your doctor or get professional medical advice before using any of the suggested remedies, techniques, or information in this book.

Upon using the information contained in this book, you agree to hold harmless the Author from and against any damages, costs, and expenses, including any legal fees potentially resulting from the application of any of the information provided by this guide. This disclaimer applies to any damages or injury caused by the use and application, whether directly or indirectly, of any advice or information presented, whether for breach of contract, tort, negligence, personal injury, criminal intent, or under any other cause of action.

You agree to accept all risks of using the information presented inside this book. You need to consult a professional medical practitioner in order to ensure you are both able and healthy enough to participate in this program.

Table of Contents

INTRODUCTION 1

CHAPTER 1: UNDERSTANDING THE TERM "CONSCIOUS PARENTING" 2

CHAPTER 2: A BETTER RELATIONSHIP WITH YOUR CHILD THROUGH POSITIVE PARENTING SOLUTIONS 8

CHAPTER 3: CHARACTERISTICS OF PRESCHOOL KIDS 14

CHAPTER 4: INSTILL VALUES EARLY 19

CHAPTER 5: STEPS TO BECOMING A PEACEFUL PARENT .. 27

CHAPTER 6: A HAPPY HOUSEHOLD: WHY EVERY PARENT SHOULD CHOOSE TO PARENT POSITIVELY 39

CHAPTER 7: WHAT IS NEURO LINGUISTIC PROGRAMMING? 54

CHAPTER 8: UNDERSTANDING YOUR RESPONSIBILITIES AS PARENTS 60

CHAPTER 9: HOW TO KNOW IF YOU ARE A FINE PARENT IN 2 MINUTES? 71

CHAPTER 10: IS IT NECESSARY TO BRING UP THE CHILDREN? 76

CHAPTER 11: LOVE 79

CHAPTER 12: COMMON MISTAKES PARENTS MAKE WHEN DISCIPLINING THEIR CHILDREN 89

CHAPTER 13: SOCIAL 96

CHAPTER 14: OLD SCHOOL V/S NEW SCHOOL MOTHERHOOD 116

CHAPTER 15: DISCOVERING YOUR OWN PARENTING PERSONALITY 129

CHAPTER 16: A NEW IDEA: PUT YOURSELF FIRST 134

CHAPTER 17: RAISING STRONG-WILLED AND SELF-CONFIDENT CHILDREN.. 140

CHAPTER 18: QUESTION OF FINANCIAL SECURITY 150

CHAPTER 19: TIPS FOR RAISING AN EMOTIONAL CHILD 156

CHAPTER 20: BEGIN THE APPROACH EARLY 173

CONCLUSION.. 182

Introduction

This book contains various steps and strategies on how to raise your teens to become the responsible and mature adults that they were meant to be.

Raising your children through the teen years is one of the most challenging responsibilities of being a parent. Skip the drama and watch your child's transition into a beautiful and well-adjusted adult. Empower yourself by learning the ins and outs of raising teenagers the easy way.

Thanks again for downloading this book, I hope you enjoy it!

Chapter 1: Understanding The Term "Conscious Parenting"

Conscious Parenting basically deals with the fostering of such values and ideas that are expected to be innately grown in children over the span of their growth and development. Conscious parenting particularly challenges the conventional methods of parenting in which there exists no firm code of behavior and standards to follow by both children and parents.

In order to become a successful conscious parent or guardian, it is vital to specify some basic fundamentals of conscious parenting which includes:

· Conscious parenting is not at all meant to contradict the traditional practices of parenting; rather it is concentrating towards the alterations in those conventional practices of parenting which fail to interpret the behavior of a child.

· The parents should adopt the attracting and uniting methods for the effective development of intelligent as well as emotional quotient among the children by replacing the reformatory and punishing methods.

· It is also essential to avoid mental barriers like how accurately or early the parents have been able to deal with their children according to the traditions and how their children should learn about being responsible as well as mature.

Comparison between Conscious &

Conventional Parenting

The conventional methods of parenting immensely differ with the conscious parenting methods. One of the most essential and primary contrast that exist between both the methods are their perspective. The conventional parents possess a command oriented viewpoint towards managing their kids while the conscious parents deeply focus on the social approach. However, their responsibilityremains the same to builda solid and trustworthy bond with their children that can ensure effective mutual understanding.

An additionalsignificant distinction exists in their viewpoint in which Conscious Parenting takes into consideration their emotions, while conventional parentinginvolves the compulsive obedience of children to their parents or guardians who understand what is correct or incorrect for them.

In conventional parenting the entire power of decision making was in the hands of the parents while conscious parenting promotes the active involvement of the child in handling different situations, and letting them be a part of the decision making.

This basically elaborates the confidence on the fact that appropriate collaboration helps with the development of strong emotional bond with the child. It should not be misunderstood that any kind of perilous activities or behavior is permitted.

In addition to these comparisons, further distinction comes with compassion, resilience, unautocratic approach and comprehension versus firmness, strict methodologyand discipline.

The days, when children were dutiful puppets for their parents are now history. Thus, Conscious Parenting contradicts the act of punishment as it becomes the major cause of barrier between parents and kids in today's world.

In fact, Conscious Parenting basically carries a superior level of maturity in its thinking to provide endless support to the children for their empowerment in terms of decision making and having a more productive behavior.

Chapter 2: A Better Relationship With Your Child Through Positive Parenting Solutions

When you decide to bring a child into this world, you take the complete responsibility of caring for that child, but often, the patience of the parents dwindles, which can have an adverse effect on the child in the long run. Positive parenting solutions act as a guide, helping your children grow in the best way, so they have a successful life – both personally and professionally. Because when your child is a good human being, they will be able to deal with the challenges life throws them in a positive way. The power of positive parenting is clear when the child grows up and reflects positivity in their own life.

Some parents are gifted with a positive nature and find patience and positive thinking come naturally, but for those who struggle with a negative temperament, positive parenting solutions can make a significant different in your parenting approach.

Smart and Helpful Positive Parenting Skills

A good parent always knows the best skills to which they can apply positive parenting and keep the relationship with their child healthy. Excellent parenting skills can be learned if you do not possess them naturally. When parents have been raised by individuals with the utmost parenting skills, they often prefer to use the same techniques on their own children. Sometimes this works, but it can't hurt to have additional solutions at the ready.

To bring out the best in your kid, as well as see them live a happy and successful life here are some of the best positive parenting skills you can incorporate into your parenting approach you can be a great parent without any extra effort if you are aware of these amazing skills.

Affection and Love

Love is one of the biggest priorities which a parent should always demonstrate with their child. It helps in supporting the child mentally and physically. Love can be developed by simply spending more time together.

Manage Your Stress

You need to know how to manage stress that comes from your home, work, and your child. Practice relaxation techniques and think positive, so your mood or routine does not affect the child.

Maintaining a Healthy Relationship

Keep in mind that you have to maintain a healthy relationship with your child, just like you do with your spouse. This isn't necessarily something that just happens. Sometimes it takes extra effort and thoughtfulness on your part.

Provide Autonomy

When you trust your child and give them the autonomy to do things their way, it helps him/her to feel confident. Treat your child with utmost respect, which will encourage him/her to share everything with you without hesitation.

Education

Provide the tools for educating your child in the best manner. Encourage him/her to seek opportunities for learning and success in life. Promote learning unconsciously, so he/she takes it seriously. Keep in mind too, every child learns differently and excel in different ways.

Life Skills

Life skills include budgeting the income

you earn to survive. Educate them about the difference between need and want so they can live resourcefully when they are adults on their own.

Behavior Skills

Use positive reinforcements to help him/her learn and make sure he/she does not fall into the trap of any negative behavior.

Healthy Lifestyle

Be a role model. Surround them with a healthy lifestyle to show them how to eat healthy, exercise, and take care of themselves emotionally and physically.

Religious Learning

Encourage them to participate in religious learning and understand its importance in life.

Protect Your Child

Keep updated on who your child's friends

and colleagues are so that you can guide them if they face any problems. Let them deal with the world themselves, but always ensure they know they can come to you for guidance.

Chapter 3: Characteristics Of Preschool Kids

Self love- A preschooler tends to think that she is the center of the world. Your youngster believes that everything on the planet spins around her.

Freedom- A preschooler will want to help with household chores and put on his clothes without help. Be quiet as your youngster practices these abilities unless there is no time.

Innovativeness- the level of imagination in your child's mind is very high. The world he lives in is full of magical ideas and fantasies.

"Why?" Preschoolers are attempting to realize about their surroundings; they will ask "why" always! Take the time to help your youngster find out about what causes the occasions happening around him.

Sociality- Preschoolers are figuring out how to be a decent partner or companion to other kids their age. Preschool, play dates, day care or playgroups give radiant chances to your youngster to learn necessary social skills.

Listening- Preschoolers should be taught how to listen to other people with interest and patience. You should model suitable listening conduct for your preschooler by effectively listening to her when she lets you know about her day, her age mates and her discoveries. That way she will learn to do the same to others.

Locomotion- Preschoolers are additionally learning complex developments, for example, jumping, climbing, and skipping. Let your youngster practice often and make it fun!

Courageousness and being adventurous- Kids can be exceptionally dynamic amid this time period. Make a point to give protective caps when riding tricycles and do general wellbeing looks out for play gear.

Pronunciation- Eloquence and pronunciation enhances during this time. Try not to be frightened if your kid forgets word sounds at times. She will soon pick up and pronounce all words properly.

Principles and standards- preschoolers are beginning to differentiate what is right or wrong. You can help by setting firm and steady limits for your youngster.

Fantasies versus dreams- Preschoolers must take in the difference between fantasy and reality. Before the end of the preschool years, your kid will have a good understanding of past, present and future.

Fears- New phobias, particularly to new sights and sounds are normal at this age. Be strong and supportive while attempting to help them overcome the fears. The fears may not go immediately, but with time they will.

Poor sportsmanship-your child will want to learn rules in games but will anyway want to emerge first position every time he participates. Eventually, he will learn how to play fair and even accept defeat

Highly impressionable- Preschoolers are vigorously affected by what they see. It's vital to effectively regulate what your kid is presented to on TV and in this present reality.

Sexual interest- It is typical for preschoolers to take part in sexual investigation. Help your youngster realize what is fit for him.

Chapter 4: Instill Values Early

In the first few years of life children learn many complex skills, behaviors and concepts. Most children learn initially how to crawl, later to roll or scoot, and ultimately they learn how to walk. Children start to communicate by making cooing noises, followed by vowel sounds and eventually by adding different pitches to their sounds. Their vocal skills will continue to develop as they say their first words around the age of one year. They will continue to add more vocabulary each year, and by the time they are seven they will have mastered all speech sounds and will be capable of carrying on a conversation with an adult. Interestingly enough, children of bilingual parents may learn how to talk in two languages at a similar pace.

Children will learn to dress, undress, feed themselves, play, ride a bike, as well as to read and write. The feats that children conquer so easily are almost unfathomable to adults faced with similar challenges. To learn to swim as an adult or to learn a foreign language may seem like a monstrous task, but to children learning and mastering new skills happens quickly and effortlessly.

During your child's early developmental years (normally prior to age seven), learning everlasting values, such as; love, good manners, respect, self-esteem and honesty can be simply mastered. Values instilled in a child during this time as they are learning to walk, talk, dress, read and write, will influence the child not only through their school years but for the rest of their lives.

Love

Providing unconditional love to your child gives them a strong feeling of security and helps them develop confidence. Love is a feeling that is demonstrated through showing affection. Telling your child you love them frequently will soon yield the response of, "I love you too." In addition, show your child how to be loving by giving affection to your friends and relatives, kissing and hugging your spouse or partner and doing all these things naturally in your child's presence.

Telling your children you love them is important, but it can become robotic, so it is just as important to show your love in as many different ways as possible. Leaving a child a note they can find in their pocket or backpack, or hiding a note for them under their pillow will delight them and surprise them. These types of small and loving gestures will help your child to be open with their affection towards you, and others they care about.

Manners

Good manners are one of the most noticeable values that either children have, or have not. I have often experienced one of my children's friends tell me, rather than ask me, that they want a drink. I am always impressed when I hear sentences such as "may I please have a drink?" I imagine other parents in similar situations take notice as well. How children behave in other people's homes can be a reflection on the parent. It is very easy to teach children to say 'please' and 'thank you', but you have to be consistent and correct them if they are not doing so. Once this becomes a habit, you will rarely need to remind your children to use their good manners.

Meaning you are sorry

Along with instilling good manners such as 'please' and 'thank you' is the word 'sorry'. 'Sorry' is a word that can be said, but may not be used with the true intended meaning. As an example, a child who is jealous of another child, (perhaps one child is getting more attention, or the child is unable to win while playing a friend at a video game); their jealousy may provoke negative behavior such as turning off the video game or pushing the other person. The child may quickly say 'sorry' as this is what they have been taught, but in these situations the child does not truly mean sorry. They are just repeating what they have learned and perhaps believe that saying sorry cancels out their negative behavior. It can also make it easier for them to do something they know is wrong, as all they then have to do is say sorry, and they feel the slate has been wiped clean. When something is deliberately done to hurt another person either verbally or physically, the child should be taught that there is a consequence beyond just saying sorry.

First you have to explain to the child that the word sorry is used when something happens that is the result of an accident. Doing something intentionally is not an accident, and this is not an acceptable behavior. Next you have to address the incident and here are several remedies in these situations which will initially need coaching from the parent. One would be for the child to offer one of their toys to the other person as an act of retribution. They could offer to help clean their room or make a small card for them and write on it that they are sorry. These carry far more impact, particularly for a younger child, and they will have a greater meaning. Once a child understands that there are consequences to their actions, you will have helped them to avoid deliberate negative actions. However, you will need to give them tools to help them in situations where they are getting frustrated so that they can avoid negative behaviors altogether.

Be consistent

As a parent, when you are consistent in these situations, you will help your children understand that there are always consequences to negative actions. This will not only help them as children but will give those foundational skills necessary later in life dealing with more complicated issues.

Being consistent in all the values you teach your child is extremely important. When boundaries or rules change, or they are not consistently applied, your child will not understand why, and will likely become confused how to act or frustrated when the way they behaved yesterday is not okay today.

Chapter 5: Steps To Becoming A Peaceful Parent

Becoming a peaceful parent is not always an easy task. The demands of modern life can mean that parents are already under stress, deadlines, and pressures even before children are thrown into the mix. Some days, it can feel like our kids are testing the limits of our patience to the breaking point.

The truth is that when we're angry, we tend to react rather than respond. Depending on the situation, reacting may put a quick stop to misbehavior, but it rarely allows for teaching moments to occur. Reacting leads to yelling, ordering children to their rooms, in-the-moment punishments, and often overlooks or ignores teaching opportunities. It's also stressful for parents! Too much anger can make parenting unenjoyable and leave you feeling out of control.

Even the most practiced of parents will have moments when calm seems far away and anger flares. In the face of these moments, it's all too easy for positive parenting strategies to go out the window. The question becomes, how can we manage our anger and stay calm so that positive parenting can take place?

Patience Is Vital – Tips and Techniques to Stay Calm in Critical Situations

Let's take a look at some mindful strategies for staying calm, finding patience, and responding rather than reacting:

1. **Make a commitment to yourself.** This is not an instant-fix tip, but it does help. Making a formal commitment to yourself that you are not going to lose your temper won't stop it from happening ever again – but over time, this consciously made commitment can help you to be more aware of what's going on situationally and internally when you lose your temper. As you gain insight into your own feelings and the parenting situations that bring them on, you can start to make more mindful choices in those frustrating moments. Don't give up. As you begin to notice your anger and become better at managing it, the effectiveness of your parenting can increase. As that increases, your child's misbehaviour will start to decrease. Decreased misbehaviour means less stress, which leads to less anger. In other

words, consistently being mindful of your frustration over time can lead to a happy snowball of more enjoyable parenting!

2. **Put it in perspective.** It can be all too easy to start worrying when children test boundaries, push buttons, or misbehave. It's not uncommon for over stressed parents to start asking questions like, 'Why are they doing this? Is it because I'm not a good parent? Am I failing somehow?' Before you know it, things have escalated to 'What if they NEVER learn? What if they end up living under a bridge?!' Try to calm down and remember that button-pushing, boundary testing, and misbehaviour are all normal. They are a healthy part of your child's attempts to experiment with and understand the world around her. Expect that these things will happen. Recognize that your job is not to eliminate such issues overnight, but to guide your children through the process of growth

and discovery that comes with learning how to function safely and healthily in the human condition. That being said, if you are worried that your child's behavior is outside the norm, seek specific guidance from your pediatrician.

3. **Take a deep breath.** Sounds simple, doesn't it? Believe it or not, taking a moment to breathe is more than just pat advice. A few calming breaths can be done in under thirty seconds, but do wonders for helping you calm down. Deep breathing delivers oxygen to your blood and brain, which can help you relax and think more clearly under stress. The few seconds or minutes you spend doing this exercise can also give you a chance to pause and collect yourself before you react. You may even want to ask your children to breathe with you.

4. **Splash water on your face.** Taking a moment to splash cold water on the face helps some people to change their internal landscape just enough to step away from the anger. However, only apply this strategy, or any strategy that requires you to step away from your children, if it is safe to do so.

5. **Add new tools to your toolbox.** Come up with a list of anger management techniques that have worked for you in the past, then go out and find some new ones to add to the list (hint: this chapter is a great place to start!). When you feel anger coming on, pull one of these 'tools' from your anger management toolbox. Simply being prepared with options when things escalate can do wonders for one's ability to regain control.

6. **Remember that feelings are contagious**. If you are angry, anxious, or

stressed, your children probably will be too. Kids are smart – even when parents control their reactions, it's likely that little ones will pick up on the fact that mom or dad is upset. This can stress children out and lead to further misbehavior, adding fuel to the fire. Taking a moment to remember that our own anger is making things worse can sometimes give us the pause we need to apply a calm-down strategy.

7. **Tip 4: Take a break.** Sometimes taking a short break can give you the space you need to regain your calm. This strategy can even be turned into a teaching moment as you model a healthy coping technique for your child. If you feel that you just can't keep it together, tell your children that you are upset and you need to take a break to calm down. Then leave (providing it is safe to do so), take a quick walk, run through some breathing exercises, do

some yoga poses – whatever helps you calm down best. When you return, you can ask your children why they thought you needed a break and jump into a teaching moment around coping with difficult emotions.

How to Stop Yelling at Your Child

A common but unfortunate side effect of anger is yelling. While yelling can sometimes put a stop to misbehavior in the moment, it's less effective in the long run for promoting discipline. It can also undermine parent-child relationships, create stress for everyone involved, and interfere with authentic attempts at communication. That being said, it's probably not the end of the world if you yell at your kids one day. It happens in most families from time to time, and beating yourself up over it is usually not helpful. Just as you want to teach your kids to learn from their mistakes and move on, if you yell at your child, learn from the experience, make amends, forgive yourself, and then move on so that positive parenting can take effect.

It should be noted that in this chapter, we are not discussing the yelling that is sometimes necessary in safety situations, such as warning your child to get out of the road in the face of an oncoming vehicle. The focus here is on yelling as the result of anger, or other negative emotions.

Let's stock up that peaceful parent toolbox a little more by looking at some tips and tricks to stop yelling:

Ask your kids to explain their feelings. It can be easy in a heated moment to feel like your child is acting out just to make you angry. Understanding the real reasons why a child has misbehaved can help add a little perspective and cool the fuse of our own anger.

It's also good for kids, who need to be heard and validated at least as much as adults do. Just listening to your child's feelings may be enough to reduce the misbehavior, which will in turn help your frustration levels.

Get a stress ball. Many people swear by these small devices. Having a stress ball to squeeze can give you something else to focus on when you're about to lose your cool, and the physical use of your hands can help take the edge off of your stress. You can try keeping one in your bag and pulling it out in heated moments.

Don't take it personally. Know that your child's misbehavior is not personal. Misbehavior is a normal part of development and to be expected as she learns to self-regulate her actions and emotions. Taking it personally will not only add to your stress in the moment, it can also lead to resentment over time.

Disengage. Until you can calm your anger, do nothing. If you've already started yelling, stop where you're at. Take a moment to calm down before you resume the interaction. The more often that you stop yourself, the more quickly you'll be to notice that you're yelling. Eventually, this strategy can help you avoid yelling altogether.

Don't force a teaching moment. Positive teaching moments can't happen when you're yelling. Wait until you've calmed down before trying to teach your child.

Take preventative action. If you know that having the plant knocked over sets you off, put it out of reach. If you know that your children's' fighting over a particular toy will lead to your yelling, put the toy away until they are ready to play without fighting. If you know that going home from the park will lead to yelling if your children refuse to come home, make a plan for how you will deal with their refusal in a more constructive way. Identifying situations that lead to yelling can help you eliminate them when appropriate and plan personal coping strategies when not.

Set realistic expectations. Frustration is more likely to occur when your kids fail to meet the behavioral expectations you've set for them. Setting expectations that are too advanced for their developmental level will only lead to 'failures' on their part and frustration for both of you. Give them – and yourself – plenty of opportunities to succeed by setting behavioral expectations that are in keeping with their developmental level.

Chapter 6: A Happy Household: Why Every Parent Should Choose To Parent Positively

The phrase "positive parenting" was by no means into circulation back when my parents were children themselves. It has sprung into popularity mainly over the past decade as professional and parents alike have discovered the vast benefits of a different method of raising and properly parenting their children. Many people believe that positive parenting is made up of a particular set of rules. But actually, it is a belief that way of living, a change in the style in which you parent, if you will. In parenting in a positive manner, one believes that children, just like adults, should be treated with respect and should not feel shamed or fear their parent's violent outbursts when disciplined. It is meant to be full of love and encouraged guidance.

Positive parenting has been around for hundreds of years. It is seen in the actions parents take to help their kids set positive goals. It is seen in the support we give our children and even as we try to relate to them. These are all great positive principles of parenting. The major difference between then and now is that children were often told what to do and how to do it by their parents, but never really given a reason why. They just knew to do what they were told, or they may be punished or spanked. That is the beauty of positive parenting; it teaches kids the "why" behind the actions they are told to perform. Parents back then controlled their kids more than they dedicated themselves to actually training their children in the way they saw fit.

That being said, I believe that parenting is a type of science. Improving the methods in which people parent may look like a daunting task, because it is. There are many competing views about what qualifies as "good parenting." But I truly believe that we can hone the behaviors that have been within our cultures for many years, one baby step at a time.

It's Never Too Late to Start Positive Parenting

If you have never done anything such as maintaining goals with your children or anything along the lines of positive parenting, this does not mean it is too late for you to start incorporating its methods into your everyday life. Yes, change is difficult. But thankfully, we human beings were built to adapt, and kids are the spitting image of this fact. If you found and are now reading this book, you are already making a great positive choice and effort to better your life in order to create the best environment you can for your kid(s) as they grow and mature.

Positive parenting not only impacts your child's life in affirmative ways, it also changes the life of the parent as well. When conducted properly, this method of parenting actually builds a solid foundation to heighten self-esteem and positively driven emotions between both the parent(s) and the child. It has been proven by various health professionals, family counselor, and psychiatrists that the relationship between the parents raising kids actually grows in a positive manner as well when implementing these practices. There is less stress when one parent does not have to worry about the other using a heavy-hand or negative techniques. Trust is heightened and issues that arise are seen more as opportunities than negative obstacles.

If those aren't reason enough to begin practicing positive parenting in your household, perhaps the fact that this style of parenting results in your kids acting and conducting themselves better, for life. Under the direction of positive parenting, children experience a greater self-esteem and strive to receive positive feedback from their parental figures. On the other hand, when you continuously scold your child, they tend to tune you out since it is a very unpleasant experience for them personally.

Children are People, Too

Back in the olden days, kids were meant to be seen, but not heard. This is no longer the case in the modern world. Positive parenting has blasted open the door to allow parents and educators of our youth to have a brand-new perspective on children in general. The new outlook makes adults look at kids as unique human beings. This means their parents and other role models in life need to do everything in their power to drive positive actions in order to develop a child's mind for success in life. In today's world, this calls for people to be vastly creative and independent, instead of simply copying the past's traditions.

That being said, some parents provide their parents too much praise. It is important to praise for true accomplishments. If parents provide their kids with a constant diet of praise for regular and mundane tasks, this will build a child's ego in negative ways. This can cause kids to become bombastic, feeling as if every action they do deserves a reward.

There are some "old-fashioned" parenting techniques that are still utilized and still work today. But corporal punishment behind closed doors and within schools has become illegal, thank goodness. This means we have had to develop a different method of leading kids in the right direction, which is more challenging but much more effective. This is where learning about positive parenting, among other methods, has become beneficial in discovering the minds of our little counterparts as they become knowledgeable of the world around them.

There are many simple tricks that if we were merely able to change our mindset, would work wonders when it comes to discipline. Much of what you will learn throughout the chapters in this book are simple things that will make you wonder why you hadn't thought and utilized them before now. There are many benefits that come along with being a positive parent. I will tell you that it is not an easy way out, that it takes hard work and dedication in order to properly practice and utilize this style of parenting. But I assure you, there is a range of both short and long-term benefits that you and your children will positively grow from!

Benefits of Positive Parenting

Positive parenting by no means lacks discipline. While as a parent you still need to correct poor or wrong behavior, there are different things you can do to successfully do this without yelling, hitting, etc. This is where learning about positive parenting can easily become one of the best parenting decisions you will ever make!

Secure Attachment

Secure attachment is the foundation for healthy development in all children. It allows the healthy building of resilience for how your child is to act during their time as an adult. It also assists in the process of superb brain development. In order to really understand this, we must get scientific for a brief moment. The human brain doesn't totally mature until we are in our twenties. Our first 3-6 years of life on this planet are absolutely crucial for the further development of our center of command. The only section of the brain that is developed when we are born is the center that conducts survival. It merely controls autonomic functioning.

It's between this stage and age four that kids really start to develop functioning that occurs in the middle area of the brain. The brain of a three-year-old is extremely organized but lacks efficiency. Once kids reach ages 5-6, they can begin to self-regulate, meaning they can manage to pause and reflect. But this process continues to mature until the brain is totally matured.

As we all learned in anatomy class, our brains cease to hold connections that are not used. You literally lose it if you do not utilize it. This means the parents have an important role in teaching coping skills and encouraging their kids to engage in empathy and creativity. If they fail to do such, the brain will develop but with weak neural connections. If kids are stressed and fearful constantly, the brain loses its ability to function at its prime.

Ability to Understand Feelings

Positive parenting thrives on the fact that you are able to openly share feelings between you and your kids.

For example, if your child decides to run across a parking lot without looking at their surroundings first, simply and calmly explain to them how that action makes you nervous and how upset you would be if they were injured in any way. They will follow your directions because they don't want you to be sad if they get hurt. This type of behavior from a parenting standpoint builds empathy between you and your child that will last a lifetime. This will also teach your child to think about the feelings of others before acting.

Decrease of Power Struggles

Disciplining your kids in harsh manners can cause them to feel shameful and poorly about themselves. They bury all of that shame of their bad behavior within themselves instead of simply correcting it, which fuels them to continuously act out in ways parents don't see fit. If you continue down this path with your child, they will see you as an obstacle, which will result in struggles for power. It's crucial to set up boundaries but do so with empathy and fairness in mind. If you treat your kids in a cruel manner, they will grow up thinking it is okay to treat others that way too.

Healthy Emotional Development

When children grow up feeling good about themselves, they will mature into someone that has a good self-esteem. They know they are easily capable of success with hard work and can truly feel good about positive accomplishments. Using harsh punishments can plant a sense of fear and shame that will later grow into them making bad decisions or surpassing making crucial decisions at all.

Uncover Motivators

All of us are motivated by different things. Children are human too, so this applies to them as well. As a parent, you only limit yourself when you use harsh punishments. If anything, you think more creatively through the means of positive parenting. When you learn how to isolate the things your child values, you can then use that to your advantage.

For example, if your teenager heavily values their independence, reward behavior you approve of by allowing them to do "grown-up" things by themselves.

Building of Strong Relationships

It is pretty obvious that positive parenting can allow plenty of room for positive relationships between family members to flourish, since they are based from accomplishments and good memories. Parents must learn the importance of learning how to set boundaries through loving guidance. This builds a circle of respect for everyone in the family. When done correctly, parents will no longer have to discipline children, but simply offer guidance when they need it. Doesn't that sound like a dream come true?

Development of Character

Through the means of positive parenting sprouts children who are motivated by the desire for excellence in their lives. They wish to behave well in order to truly reach their goals, not because they are fearful of being punished if they don't do as such. This means that when they grow up, they are able to monitor their results and themselves as they seek opportunities to do well in all the things they do.

I am sure that you can see that the benefits of positive parenting far outweigh the negatives, because there are no consequences to implementing and utilizing this method of parenting! That being said, the next chapter shall shed some light on the most important part of successfully parenting in a positive manner: the parent(s) themselves!

Chapter 7: What Is Neuro Linguistic Programming?

NLP stands for Neuro Linguistic Programming and it refers to:

Neuro, which is everything, that goes on in our head.

Firstly we have **values** about what is important to us and our family; the rules we live by. We have inherited them from our own parents and are usually attracted to a partner in life who holds the same values.

What are the values you want to live by as a family and how are you passing these on to your children in what you say and do, on a daily basis?

Secondly we have beliefs and these may well be different from our parents and our partner, as they will be based on our life experiences, knowledge, reading, travelling and our education. They are the things we hold to be true. Children believe everything we say when they are very young but as we know only too well, this doesn't last for long as they learn that we are not perfect and all knowing!

Beliefs change constantly as we learn more about the world, get disillusioned and start to realise that things are not 'black or white' but can be shades in between.

Some of our beliefs help us on our way and enable us to do what we want in life and these are called 'resourceful beliefs'. These are the 'I can's. Then there are the 'limiting beliefs' which are the 'I can't's.

Notice the resourceful beliefs your children have and encourage these because these beliefs will help them overcome the less resourceful ones.

Beliefs and values — the neuro bit, underpin what we say and do which is the next part.

Linguistic is how we communicate, what we say and what we tell ourselves (that mischievous inner voice). The words we choose reflect how we experience the world.

We may use more visual words to reflect our visual preference such as 'see', 'imagine', 'look' for example. Visual communicators tend to speak quickly and have a higher pitch, they also look up as they search their mind for the visual reference.

If we are more auditory then we focus more on what we hear and sue words like 'listen', 'sound', 'noise'. We talk slower and lower, looking down slightly.

If we are more kinaesthetic, we notice feelings and actions and use a lot of 'doing words' like 'get', 'take' 'do'. We may use our hands to express ourselves and move around as we talk. It's difficult to keep still.

As far as possible it's a good idea to match the preference of the person we want to get on with. So if you want your child to do what you've asked, it's best to use their preference.

By changing some of the words we use with our children and teenagers, our pitch and pace and our body language we can achieve what we want without shouting at them, getting stressed or becoming upset.

Programming is what happens next! It is the result and patterns of behaviour we get from how we think and what we say.

We need to focus on when we **do** get the results we want and understand how we got them. What was the 'code' or structure? It's about the process rather than the content, the 'how' rather than 'what'. We can then replicate it to get the desired result again rather than repeating the language or behaviour that produced the undesirable result or no result.

"If you always do what you've always done you will always get what you've always got"

NLP is used a lot in the business world to enhance sales and leadership skills as part of Management Training but arguably parents have more need of these skills because we are training the next generation.

You will be a happier parent when you understand how **you** can get the change you want from your children by showing them and being the change yourself.

Chapter 8: Understanding Your Responsibilities As Parents

It is the responsibility of all parents to keep their children safe. We, as parents, share this responsibility with other members of our community. Others who share in the responsibility include, but not limited to, babysitters, daycare workers, teachers, coaches, resource officers, emergency personnel, and service providers that we trust with our most valuable resources.

It is the responsibility of each parent to ensure that you only allow responsible, reliable, and trustworthy people to care for your children when you are not present. A simple background check on a potential babysitter and asking for references are simple steps you can take to ensure your child is in good hands. Most neglect and child abuse, along with sexual abuse, on children of all ages are committed by a family member or a family friend.

While your child is at school, involved in sports or other activities, or in the company of other professionals, never simply trust that they are in good hands. You can request information on professionals and even do a public record check on basically anyone. It is also advised that you conduct unannounced visits as often as possible. And talk regularly with your child to ensure you know what is going on with them.

When your child is an infant, toddler, or young child, it is your responsibility to ensure your child is left unattended. Many parents use a baby monitor to assist them with monitoring infants. If you choose to use a monitor, ensure that the batteries are fresh and strong and do regular checks to make sure it is working properly. Also, with any monitor use, make sure you always know the range of the monitor and remain within the range.

Some parents allow older children to assist in caring for the younger children. It is your responsibility to determine if the older child is mature and responsible enough to properly care for the younger child. Age has nothing to do with a child's ability to assist in the care of a younger child. A child may have a mentality that is much lower than their actual age in years. The same is true for adults you may be considering for the job.

Parents are responsible for providing a proper home environment for their children. Your home needs to have an environment that makes your child feel loved, safe, and comfortable. No one can create tat environment for child except you.

Parents are responsible for providing food for their children. This may sound like common sense to some, but many parents are not aware of the what is in the foods they buy and what essential nutrients their children may be lacking. A child's diet can drastically impact their growth, their health, their mood, their behavior, and their mental health. It is the parent's responsibility to ensure their children receive the proper nutrients for every stage of growth.

Providing proper clothing is another area where parents are responsible. Children require clothing that protects them from the elements. When it is cold, children need clothing that keeps them warm. When it is hot, children need clothing that keeps them cool. The selected clothing does not need to be a certain brand or come from an expensive store. Clothing should be clean and provide the coverage intended.

Ensuring your child receives a proper education is a responsibility that far too many parents neglect. Too many parents think that if they send their children to school that they are meeting their responsibility. This couldn't be further from the truth. It is a proven, documented fact that when parents are involved with their child's education, the child does better in school, make better grades, and are less likely to drop out of school. As a parent, you can make sure your child has done their homework, check over the work, and pay attention to all work and notices brought home by your child.

Other areas of involvement in your child's education would be for you to volunteer to assist with any activities at your child's school. You can accompany your child on field trips. You can also set up regular meetings with your child's teachers to stay informed of all progress your child is making and be aware of any areas your child may need help in. How you treat your child's education at a young age will pave the road that your child will travel in life. If you make education important in your family, the pattern will continue for your child's family.

Medical neglect is a major issue in the United States. It is the responsibility of every parent to ensure their child receives the medical attention they need. With medical costs on the rise and medical care being so expensive, children's heath needs are sometimes neglected. If you cannot afford medical screenings, regular check-ups, and needed medical care for your child, it is your responsibility to apply for assistance with healthcare.

Healthcare in America has become one of the top political issues among politicians, big donors, big pharmaceutical companies, and political parties. This is nothing new. Each state has different programs that work to assist those without heath-coverage. However, not every person is covered, even with the assistance programs in place. If you cannot afford care and you do not qualify for the state assisted programs, most areas have state run Health Departments where a person is charged based on their income.

It is the responsibility of every parent to ensure their child is aware of safety rules and precautions. The most basic rule for small children is to never talk to stranger or accept any candy or gifts from anyone they do not know. Children should be taught that they must tell a trusted adult if any person makes them feel uncomfortable or acts in anyway that does not feel acceptable.

Another safety issue that parents are responsible for is the child being safe from the infestation of drugs. Sadly, drug use by parents is the number one reason children are removed from their parents by the courts in most areas of the U.S. With that being said, there is a pretty high chance that your child will be in contact with children who have been exposed to drug use in their home. You cannot depend on the basic "Just Say No to Drugs" lessons that are commonly taught in schools to educate your child on the dangers of drugs.

As your children grow into pre-teens and teenagers, they will start to demand some freedoms and independence. This is normal and should be encouraged. These small steps into the real world is what helps them adjust into adulthood. However, this is not the time to slack on your responsibilities and ignore what your children are doing with their newfound freedom and independence.

It is your responsibility to check-up on what your child is doing, where they are going, who they are with, and what time they are to be home. You must set responsible boundaries and ensure that those boundaries are kept in place. Pre-teens and teenagers, by their very nature, will test the boundaries you set simply to see if they can ignore your rules without notice or consequences.

Today, as is evident by the rise in juvenile delinquency, the word "NO" has become obsolete in many homes. However, as a responsible parent, it is your job to say no.

If your child is making friends with people you do not trust or who you feel is a bad influence on their behavior, just say no. If your child is going places that you do not like or places that are having a negative impact on their behavior, just say no. When your children are getting older you may feel that you want to be their "friend". There is nothing wrong with that, if you do not stop being the parent at the same time.

Our children are our future. You can never go wrong investing your time, love, and energy in a child. Although this book focuses on the RESPONSIBILITIES of the parents, you must remember that you are blessed with the PRIVILEGE of guiding your children into their future. Your responsibilities, if taken seriously and applied effectively, is the primary guide your children will use throughout their lives. What your child accomplishes, how they act and behave, and what they become is a direct result of how you provide parenting to your children. Your parenting responsibilities should never be taken lightly.

Chapter 9: How To Know If You Are A Fine Parent In 2 Minutes?

What makes a fine parent? Are you doing good in your new role as a mother or a father? These simple questions may seem easy to answer, but they also provoke thinking about your parenting style and gauge how are you as a parent.

Let's say you only have 2 minutes to answer and the clock starts now!

Questions to ask yourself:

What is your concept of "discipline"?

Does it work?

Which techniques are you going to keep?

Which strategies are you going to let go?

What new tricks will you try?

How do rate yourself? Do you think or believe that you are a fine parent? There is no right or wrong answer to the given questions. Whether you give yourself a thumbs up or a thumbs down, the fact remains that you are now responsible for nurturing the growth and development of a precious child. You don't need to be perfect to become a fine parent. Your child is not perfect, too, so don't set your expectations too high that you would neglect the most essential aspect of parenting- building and enjoying a healthy, happy, and open relationship with him.

A Fine Parent

The concept of a fine parent revolves on how you provide the essential needs for his optimum development – food, shelter, love, and discipline. If you can provide the perfect balance of all these factors, you can say that you are a fine parent. And when the child grows with adequate food for nourishment, living in a decent abode, well-loved by the family, and given a positive form of discipline, he will turn into a fine adult.

To become a fine parent, avoiding the dangers of abuse, overindulgence, or neglect is not enough. You have to focus on the following major responsibilities as delineated by The National Academy of Sciences:

Maintain your child's health and safety

Promote his emotional health and well-being

Prepare your child intellectually

Instill social skills

Various studies attested to the fact that parents who combined sensitivity and warmth, along with clear behavioral expectations, raised well-adjusted children. They practiced the Four C's of parenting:

Care – showing affection and affection

Consistency – maintaining a healthy, safe, and stable environment

Choices - allowing the child to develop self-autonomy

Consequences – applying the repercussions of choices, whether negative or positive

However, it is also true that even if the child has everything, there are circumstances that can cause problems. It happens when he is exposed to extremely difficult situations, harsh environment, peer pressure, and traumas. Any of these factors alter the character or personality of a person, whether he is a child, a teen, or a young adult.

It is also important to accept the fact that every child is unique and grows up differently from his siblings. If they grow up fine, you can proudly claim that you are a fine parent. If you have done everything for them to become independent and responsible individual, you are a fine parent. Even if at some point in your life, you and your child encounter rough moments that somehow make you question your parenting skills, they are not enough reasons to say that you are not a fine parent.

Sometimes, how your child turns out when he becomes an adult is beyond your control. Even if you supplied him with the vital four factors, genetics and environment would influence his development. Do not blame yourself. Assess the whole situation, accept what you cannot change, and continue giving him your unconditional love. It is the best quality of a fine parent.

Chapter 10: Is It Necessary To Bring Up The Children?

Often people see the upbringing as the imposition of their tastes, requirements, tasks, plans, and dreams, like, **'I bring him up the way he must grow, I know what he should be aware, what he should do.'** If someone sees upbringing in this way, my attitude to this is negative, and I would choose another word: help in a child's development, formation, nurturing.

It Is Still Important to Learn

How to Conduct a Dialogue with the Child?

Carl Rogers said that 'an adult on a child could be compared to a gardener helping a plant. The gardener's job is to supply water, provide the facility with the sunlight, fertilize the soil. That is, to create conditions for development but not to pull the top.' **If someone sees upbringing in this way, my attitude to this is negative, and I would choose another word: help in a child's development, formation, nurturing.**

Dialogue is a bit narrowed concept, I'd better say, mutual understanding, the mood for understanding the child. Yes, it is essential to know his parent, but the parent can find out more about his childhood. And what does it mean to understand the child? First and foremost, its ways to know his needs and to take them into account. The person's needs vary not only with age but individually, depending on the child's trajectory. Therefore, it is essential to hear the child in a dialogue, understand why he doesn't listen to you, and the reasons for his refusals and rudeness. If your discussion includes 'to hear,' I accept it.

I reject any rough interpretations of the word **'upbringing'** like if a child doesn't listen, force him; if he talks rudely, corrects him; if he is offended, tell him, **'there is nothing to be offended here, you are to blame for what has happened."**

Chapter 11: Love

Love can be difficult to define in words but it is easy to show through your actions. In fact, you can show your child love every day without ever being accused of spoiling them.

Love Is Not:

Material things that you buy your child

Taking your child out to eat

Spending money on something they want

Taking them on vacation to somewhere fun or exciting

Love above all else is not materialistic. It is not about you, but about the one you love. Love is about being selfless in both your attitudes and actions.

What is Love?

When I try to define love, I try to remember the relationship or marriage two people will have and how that relationship will last over the years through thick and thin. It doesn't matter if they experienced emotional turmoil, money troubles or just had a good time through it all. That couple made it loving each other and showing their children that love. It didn't matter how hard things were for this couple, love endured.

Love is not only about taking care of others, but putting responsibility ahead of the things we want to do, the fun things. Responsibility ensures that a family is safe and that the basic necessities such as shelter, food, water and money come in. Having fun and spending money often results in a family loses what they need and that is not love but impulse and greed.

Raising Your Child with Love

Never withhold hugs and kisses. It will not spoil your child to tell them that you love them or even hug and kiss them when they are around you. A spontaneous, surprising hug will mean more than a deliberate, "afterthought" type of hug.

Be in contact with your child whenever you can. Sometimes the simple gesture of a physical touch can show love and help your child become a positive, loving person. A flip of a girl's hair, a hand on the back of the neck for reassurance, holding hands, snuggling on the couch watching TV, and any other simple contact will strengthen the positive bond between you and your child.

Show affection with your spouse around your children. Again, simple touches, rubbing one's head, giving a short massage, holding hands, and quick kisses on the cheeks or lips are acceptable for your child to see. This contact reassures your child that it is normal, loving, and worth having in their life.

Spending Time with Your Child

It is important to spend time with your child as part of the positive parenting process. For example, when you come home from work do you:

A: Walk in the door, your child rushes to you, you pick them up, give them hugs and kisses, and maybe even spin around.

B: Walk in the door, your child rushes to you and you brush them aside or tell them "Hi, I'm busy, I have work to do"."

Which situation sounds like a home with displaying a positive environment and loving relationship? If you chose situation A, you would be correct. It seems like common sense, but there are plenty of parents who come home only to ignore their children.

It is important to have a balance between your work responsibilities and your family responsibilities. You have to maintain a healthy balance and spend time with your children in order to foster that positive growth. Your children should be the priority so much that it becomes routine.

A good way to start the routine of spending time with your children is to eat breakfast together. Of course, this also means that you'll have to get up earlier so be sure that you set the appropriate bedtime for both you and your child.

A good rule of thumb is that most children should be in bed by 8pm, in order to wake up at 6am for a proper morning routine and breakfast.

When your child is old enough, school will occupy most of their day. If your child is younger, they may have day care or preschool to keep them busy while you're working.

After their daytime activities, you should pick them up and help them with any assignments or schoolwork. Making a healthy dinner and having some down time in the evening between bed-time is also important.

Spending time with your children doesn't mean that you have to do something fun all the time either. Yes, it is great if you come home, play around, and snuggle while watching TV, but, don't forget that there are other responsibilities that shouldn't be neglected like household chores.

Including your children in household chores is a good way to ensure you spend time with them how to be responsible and provide love. There is nothing wrong with getting a chair set up by the sink and having help washing the dishes or having your child clear the table or put dishes in the dishwasher. Your child can learn to help you with daily chores as soon as they learn to walk.

The best part? Since you will be right beside them, they still get your love, affection, and attention, without it always being about fun.

Balancing free time with responsibilities is essential to positive parenting and showing your child that love is not just about the fun times or the affectionate times. Love is a balance between the two.

Exercises for Love

Maybe you are not the most expressive person in the world or you have trouble expressing yourself clearly. It can happen to the best of us. It could be that you are hesitant to show love because of your own negative experiences during childhood or maybe you just never saw love expressed by your own parents. Regardless, your children will need you to express your love for them.

If you have trouble expressing yourself, you can practice! Just like anything in life, practice makes perfect and you can practice being more kind and loving. Obviously, you show emotions to your spouse but you need to practice showing appropriate emotions to your children too.

If you know you usually have a defficulty in showing emotions, have your spouse help you open up around your children. Your spouse can help simply by being more affectionate with you and by providing support in front of your children. These behaviors will help remind you that you need to be more emotionally available in front of your children. A good way to improve the way you express your emotions is to rehearse them. Think about how you'll approach your children when you wake up, get home from work and throughout your interactions. Imagine walking into the room with a smile on your face, picking up your child and giving hugs and kisses. After a while the discomfort you feel from showing your emotions will ease.

You may always need to remind yourself that showing your love through touch, smiles and words are important for your child, but you can do it.

On the other hand, if you are very expressive with your emotions you may also need a reminder that balance is part of the equation. Love can be as much about discipline and responsibility as it can be about fun and free time. It is also about being consistent from the moment your child is born.

Chapter 12: Common Mistakes Parents Make When Disciplining Their Children

Making of mistakes is inevitable when raising children. As such, in order to avoid making the same common mistakes now and then, it is helpful we identify the mistakes that we make and learn on what we can do about them.

Lack of Setting of rules

Parents fail at this. You want your child to follow simple instructions and behave well yet you have not laid down a solid foundation. Rules are very important as they act as a guidance for the child of what they should or should not do. They also act as a reminder to the child who is prone to forget easily. Lack of planning on your side leads to indiscipline. It is important that you set your house rules earlier from the time your child is mature enough to understand what you tell them. Also, it may be advisable to set the rules with the help of your child so that they can feel like they are a part of the rules they set.

Bad role models

As parents, we mostly lack the ability to be role models to our children. This is so in the sense that we set some rules that should be observed in the family but see it as okay when we violate them. When our children do the opposite, we become offended and punish them forgetting that we are supposed to guide them in doing the right things. For instance, if the rule is honesty at all times, if your child discovers that you lied about something or made a promise that you did not keep, they will think that it is okay to lie and thus will embrace such behavior. Additionally, our negative attitude towards other people or things may also affect our child's behavior.

If you are disrespectful to the cleaner, gardener or waiter at the restaurant, then your child will think that it is okay to be disrespectful to others. Therefore, if you want your child to be respectful, then you need to lead by example by being respectful too.

Absentee Parents

We cultivate negative behavior in our children when we become absent in most part of their lives. Children are supposed to be monitored and guided on a daily basis if you want them to grow responsibly. So, what happens in the current society? Parents have become too engrossed in their careers such that they treat their jobs as the first priority; in the process, children end up being neglected. This results in children engaging in activities such as drinking, smoking, stealing and use of abusive language as how can you identify bad behavior to correct it when you are not around? However busy you may be, you still need to find time for your children to instill the right behavior and correct them when they go wrong at an early age.

Setting too high expectations

Seldom do we sit back and try to reason if the expectations that we have set for our children can be achieved or not. We forget that children are in their growing stage hence they are to achieve set goals slowly as they mature. From education, to sports to household chores, we expect our children to be perfect, have perfect grades, participate, and do well in a sport and clean the dishes spotlessly. When they fall short of our expectations, we end up punishing them. Yeah, expectations are good but as a parent you should know your limits, by pushing the child too far, they will cease to obey you hence end up participating in uncouth behaviors.

Making comparisons

Children are unique in their own way. At times, as parents, we fail to understand this when we see our children performing poorly in some areas. You then end up making comparisons using an older or younger sibling and even the next-door neighbor's children; for instance telling your child, "If only you could play football like Peter or Sarah." When you do so, the child may never feel that they are good at anything and may struggle to please you. In most cases, they will shy off from taking responsibilities for fear of failing. Giving words of encouragement is what is needed to boost your child's morale and achieving set goals.

Becoming too flexible and changing with circumstances

This is the biggest mistake of all times. To be a good parent, you have to incorporate consistency in what you say or do on a daily basis. This applies when being a role model to your child, setting rules, expectations, creating time to spend with your child and so on. Children can be able to tell when you are not true to your words or actions. They need to see that what was said yesterday remains to be so as they grow up to avoid confusion. For instance, creating a policy of no watching television before doing the homework or house chores should be maintained throughout the child's life without compromise and excuses. Chosen consequences of our child's unacceptable behavior should always be practiced. Be consistent in your parenting and all the puzzles of discipline and responsibility will fall into place.

While we have emphasized a lot on instilling discipline and responsibility on your children by embracing Zen parenting, we have not looked at how instilling discipline and responsibility can benefit your children not only now but also many years to come. Let us now look at how your children can benefit from effective Zen parenting that instills responsibility and discipline.

Chapter 13: Social

Raise Your Kids Around Positive Minded People

The environment in which a child is raised influences their future conduct a lot. Kids easily pick up the behaviour and actions of the people around them. If you raise your child around people who use offensive language, then your child has a higher chance of growing up to use offensive language. If you raise your child around violent people, then your child may grow to become an aggressive person in future but if you raise your child around well-mannered people, then your child will just grow up to become a well-mannered and disciplined child.

As a parent, you should be very cautious of the people who surround your child, as they are the people most likely to influence your child's future behaviour. If you do not like the way certain people conduct themselves around your baby, then you should limit or altogether cut their contact with your baby. If for instance your child's nanny does not conduct herself well around your child, do not hesitate to fire her.

How to improve your child's self esteem

Children start to develop their sense of self when they see themselves as babies through the eyes of the parents. Your kids absorb your body language, your tone of voice, and your every expression. Their self-esteem is affected by your words and actions, more than anything else.

Praising achievements, no matter how small, will go a long way towards making them feel proud. Allowing them to do things independently will make your kids feel strong and capable. On the other hand, comparing them unfavorably with another child or using belittling comments will make your child feel worthless. Avoid using words as weapons or making loaded comments. Statements such as "You behave more like a baby than your little sister!" or "What a silly thing to do!" cause just as much damage as physical blows. Be compassionate and choose your words carefully. Your child should know that everyone makes mistakes, and even when you do not condone their behavior, you still love them.

Signs of healthy and unhealthy self-esteem

Your kid's self-esteem will fluctuate as he or she grows. It is usually changed and fine-tuned through his/her experiences and new points of view. As such, it helps to be familiar with the signs of both unhealthy and healthy self-esteem.

Generally, children with low self-esteem tend to shy away from trying new things, and may talk negatively about themselves: "What is the point anyway? Nobody cares about me." Or "I will never learn to do this." Or "I'm stupid." They may get frustrated easily, give up easily or wait for someone else to take over. They are usually easily disappointed and overly critical of themselves.

If your child has low esteem, he/she will see temporary challenges as permanent and intolerable conditions, and will experience a sense of pessimism. This can increase their risk for mental health conditions and stress, as well as difficulties solving various kinds of challenges and problems they encounter.

On the other hand, if your child has a healthy self-esteem, they will exhibit joy interacting with others. They enjoy group activities and are comfortable in social settings. They are able to work towards finding a solution to rising challenges, as well voice their discontent without belittling anyone, including themselves. For instance, a child with a healthy self-esteem will say, "I don't get this," instead of snapping out, "I am an idiot." They are sure of their strengths and weaknesses, and acknowledge them. They hover a sense of optimism.

Consider your compliments

Young kids tend to require plenty of encouragement, whether they are learning to draw a circle, throw a ball or crawl. But when your child gets used to being complimented on a job well done every time he/she does something good, they may have a difficult time recognizing when they have done something worth celebrating. Your child will also sense when you are exaggerating, and may start disregarding your compliments. Avoid praising your child after doing something he/she is supposed to do. For instance, when she throws her clothes into the hamper or brushes her teeth, a simple "thank you" is enough. Be specific with your compliments. Rather than simply stating that their drawing is marvelous, you might point out her nice use of violet.

Do not rescue your child

It is a natural tendency for a parent to prevent their child from feeling discouraged, getting hurt, or making mistakes. However, intervening is not doing your child any favor. Children need to understand that it is okay to fail, and it is normal to feel angry, anxious, or sad. Overcoming obstacles will teach them to succeed. It is particularly vital for kids to get the chance to take risks or play without feeling that their parents will correct or criticize them for doing something wrong. When need be, you are encouraged to make your own little mistakes on purpose in order to make your child feel much better.

Let your kid make decisions

Giving your child the chance to make their own choices from an early age will give him confidence in his/her own good judgment. Kids obviously love to run the show, but giving them too much control can be exhausting. The best approach is to give your child 2 or 3 options to select from. For instance, instead of asking your 3 year old child what he/she wants for lunch; offer jelly, peanut butter and pasta. At the same time, have them know that certain decisions are up to you.

Concentrate on the half full glass

If your little one tends to feel overwhelmed by disappointments, help him become more optimistic. For instance, if he is behind his classmates in reading, explain to him that everyone learns at their own pace, and offer to spend your spare time reading with him.

Nurture his/her special interests

Try exposing your child to various activities, and then encourage him when he discovers something that he really loves. Children who have a passion, be it cooking or dinosaurs, feel proud of their proficiency, and have a higher chance of being successful in other areas of their lives. Unique hobbies can be particularly useful for children who find it difficult to fit in at school. You can also help your child use his special interest to connect with other children. For instance, if he is into drawing, but most of the boys in his class love sports, you could encourage him to try sports drawings. Alternatively, he could design a book about his artwork, and then present it to the class.

Encourage problem solving

When kids are able to negotiate getting something they want, they become more confident. Studies have shown that you can teach a very young child how to deal with problems by herself. The secret is to hold your tongue. For instance, if your son comes to you and tells you that a kid took his car at the playground, ask him what he thinks should be a good approach. Even if his first response is to grab the car, ask him what he thinks would be the consequence. Then ask him to think of other ways to get the car back to avoid that happening.

Look for ways to help others

Children tend to feel more confident when they feel like they are making a difference, like taking cupcakes to a nursing home or passing out plates at preschool. It is useful for children to have their own responsibilities in the house, but it is even more empowering for them to help you with a project.

Incorporate some time for your child to spend with adults

While children love hanging out with their friends, it is also important for them to spend some time with some grownups. This will expand his/her world, provide him/her with different ways of thinking, and force him/her to talk to adults other than you. It has also been shown that having a close relationship with a certain grownup, be it a friend's parent, a babysitter, an uncle or a teacher, gives children more resilience.

Fantasize about the future

When children envision themselves doing what they want to do when they grow up, or doing something important, it is bound to give them more confidence now. Discuss with your child how you, your partner, and a few other adults chose your careers. Your kid may be dreaming of being an astronaut or a pop star, but don't try to lower her expectations. The most important thing is that she is thinking about her goals.

Catch kids being good

How many times do you react negatively to your child in a given day? In some cases, the number of times you criticize your kid may be more than the compliments. How would you feel when your boss treated you with the same amount of negative guidance? A more effective approach is to time your child doing something good:

"You cleaned your room without being asked – that is terrific!" or "I'm glad to see how patient you were when playing with your sister." These comments will help encourage good behavior as opposed to constant scolding. Make a point of looking for something new to praise your child every day. Be liberal with rewards – your compliments, hugs and love are usually enough, and can work wonders. With time, you will see your child developing the kind of behavior that is desirable.

Make time for your kids

Modern lifestyle has made it difficult for kids and parents to share a family meal together leave alone spending quality time together. But kids would like nothing more. Wake up ten minutes earlier so you can have breakfast with your son, or place the dishes in the sink after dinner and take a walk with your daughter. Children who do not get sufficient attention from their parents tend to misbehave or act out, as this is a sure way to be noticed.

If necessary, you can schedule together time with your kids. Incorporate a special night every week to be alone with your kids, and let them decide what to do. Find other ways to connect, like placing a note in their lunchbox. Adolescents are seemingly less in need of undivided attention as compared to younger kids. Since there are generally fewer chances for you to connect with your teen, you should do your best when your kid does express a desire to participate in family activities or talk. Attending games, concerts and other events with your child communicates that you care, and gives you the opportunity to learn more about your child and his/her friends. Do not despair if you are a working parent. Your kids will remember the several little things you do, such as window shopping, playing cards and making popcorn.

Be a good role model

Little kids learn how to act mainly by observing their parents. Generally, younger kids tend to take more cues from you. Before you lush out in front of your child, consider this: is this the kind of behavior you want your child to exhibit when he/she is angry? Keep in mind that your kids are constantly watching you. Research has shown that children who flare up usually have an aggressive role model at home. Model the attributes you desire to see in your child: tolerance, kindness, honesty, friendliness, and respect. Exhibit selflessness. Do things for others without expecting something in return. Offer compliments and express thanks. Most importantly, treat your child the way you would want other people to treat you.

Make communication a priority

It is naïve to expect your child to do something simply because you "say so". They expect and deserve explanations in the same way adults do. If you don't take the time to explain, your child will start questioning your motives and values, and whether they have any point. Reasoning with your kid will help them learn and understand in a nonjudgmental manner. Be clear with your explanations. If there is a problem, express your feelings, describe it, and allow your child to work with you in finding a solution. Remember to include consequences. Offer choices and make suggestions. Be open to their suggestions as well. Discuss. When your child participates in your decisions, he/she will be more inspired to carry them out.

Express unconditional love

As a parent, you are responsible for guiding and correcting your child. The manner in which you articulate your corrective guidance will make all the difference in how your kid receives it. When it comes to confronting your child, avoid faultfinding, criticizing, or blaming, which can lead to resentment and undermine self-esteem. Rather, strive to encourage and nurture, even when instilling discipline. Let them understand that although you expect better behavior next time, your love is unconditional no matter what.

Try to bond with your child

A close parent-child relationship is the best way to ensure that you raise your child well. If you bond with your child at an early age, it will be difficult to break the bond even when the child grows older. By bonding with your child, you will be able to monitor their life on daily basis. If someone hurts or harms your child, your child will definitely report to you thus allowing you to take the right action.

A child who greatly bonds with parents is more likely to have a more social life. Children who trust their parents are more likely to have a healthier relationship with other people and hence have a more social life. As said, charity begins at home. A child who feels free to talk to his or her parents will feel more free to make friends and hence have a healthy social life.

There a several ways in which you can bond with your child, these include:

Spending time with your child: Even if you are too busy with your career, always make time to be with your child. You can take your kids on a road trip to get to know each other or even organize a date with them. Spending time with your child makes you understand them better and even know their weaknesses. By knowing their weaknesses, you will be able to help them overcome them and grow to stronger and more confident people in life.

Deliberately touch your child. This can be inform of hugs, wrestling matches, stroking their hair, goodnight kisses and even squeezing their hands when walking around with them. This makes them to feel loved and hence experience a sense of security when you are around and hence an easy bonding.

Take care of your child's needs: a parent who provides for a child's needs bonds easier with the child than one who neglects the child.

Things not to do that may affect your child's social life

Calling them names

As a parent, you are your child's biggest inspiration. If you abuse , call them names and even tell them that they are useless, that's the way they will always see themselves in the society and among their peers and hence they may end up being introverts and completely refusing to socialise with other kids

Lying to your child and giving excuses every time they want to spend time with you

Kids want to spend time with their parents because of various reasons. Some seek attention while others just want to spend time with their parents. Never lie to your child for whatever reason. Lying to your child makes them to lack trust in other people and this may destroy their ability to effectively make friends since they will always be convinced that if their parents always lie to them then their friends won't be any better.

Denying your child play

Some parents are either too lazy or just irresponsible and do not want to let their child play since they do not want to do dirty laundry. Denying your child play deprives them the chance to have a social life; most kids make friends in the playground and if you do not let them interact with their peers, then you might just be cultivating a way in which your child will grow up to become an anti-social being.

Disciplining your child too harshly

Everyone makes mistakes and therefore, when your child makes one, you should punish him or her with love. Punishing your child harshly may make them feel less loved and they therefore will not have a normal life as other kids.

Take your child to school

If you want to raise and give your child a better future, then take him or her to school. It is only through education that a child can have a better life. Always help your child with his studies and follow up on your child's academic performance.

Chapter 14: Old School V/S New School Motherhood

We've got more fancy technology. We've got all the information available online. But does that make the modern mothers a Supermom or just over confident that they can handle whatever comes their way? When we look back at our own childhood, there are some really sharp contrasts in history.

Mothers back in the day would ensure that they were visiting the doctor and getting the information they required. Nowadays, we end up on Google trying to decipher our symptoms before rushing to the doctor. Who needs to waste time and fuel when we can do our own research and figure things out by ourselves, right? Wrong! The generation of mothers today is so heavily reliable on technology and gadgets, they take things for granted. Now, I have nothing against gadgets. They're good, make life easier but when it comes to motherhoods, would you prefer being a hands on Mom, getting the right information from your doctor rather than reading a few words online written by people who probably have no clue what you are going through and would have had an entirely different situation from what you are going through? Ever thought about it?

Research has shown that new mothers, who often use gadgets as a source to make parenting easier, find it difficult to have a hand on approach to parenting. This, therefore results in using gadgets for everything; i.e. when the child comes of age, a parent would find it easier to keep the child busy with gadgets (like an iPad etc..) rather than spend some quality time with the child. If we take a look outside, how many children do we get to see playing or riding a bike? Not as many as we would probably come across when we were kids. Isn't that disappointing?

Old school Supermoms would head to work, return to cook up a scrumptious meal and stand at the door yelling for their kids. Modern day moms end up dialing their children on their cellular phone to call them back home for dinner. Notice the difference. Old school parenting meant knowing where your child was and what he/she was doing and who were his/her friends who they would be hanging out with, and they didn't need gadgets. In today's world, with the arrival of social media and smart phones, we don't know anything about our kids. Who their friends are and where they've been. We know absolutely nothing!

Dr. Stephanie Rosenberg, a pediatrician based in New York City has been practicing since 1984. She feels that pediatricians are last on the list of modern day mothers. A lot of mothers these days follow information that does not come from very reliable or proper sources. While visiting your child's podiatrist can help you gain more knowledge about your child's health and behavior, there are several other key areas of parenting which are undeniably harder, like getting a full meal on the dinner table and sitting together to have a meal.

The lost practice of sitting together at the dining table and having a proper meal seems to be lost these days. Instead, working mothers are alright with their children sitting in front of the television or even if the family is gathered together at the table, everybody will be busy with their phones. Responding to e-mails, busy 'liking' pictures and status updates on social media. Sounds familiar, doesn't it? When was the last time your family, and by that I mean every member of the family sat down together for a meal at the table with absolutely no gadgets being brought out every second? Don't remember, do you. With modern day mothers working hard at their job, it gets difficult for them to come home and cook up a proper healthy meal for the family. Not only do the children suffer but at the same time, you lose precious time which you could spend bonding with the children. Think about it, if there is no proper food at the table and neither members of the family sit together to eat, how are you going to bond with your children? This however, not only applies to modern Moms but also to the other parent who is helping in raising the child/children.

As a child, growing up I remember sitting down to a lovely meal with my family. Dinnertime with my kids now is different. I was always amazed how my Mom worked part-time, helped all four of us with our homework and even managed to come and help out fund-raising campaigns organized by the school. As a working woman, I tend to be more interested in my workplace and my career goals, unlike my mother who always wanted to have a beautiful home with good food on the table. But I believe, the reason we give into most or all of our children's whims and fancies is because we have higher expectations and we are not really satisfied by just having a good home with some home cooked food on the table like our Moms. While all of us mother's probably feel the same even today, our circumstances are different. Today several of us are struggling and fed up with the expectations of having to juggle everything on a daily basis. While some of us are blessed with spouses and partners who are willing to share in the daily household chores, some of us aren't all that lucky.

Another thing we notice with modern Moms is them having absolutely zero tolerance or patience for a crying toddler or a changing teenage child. And when faced with a situation, they would prefer letting the child sit with a gadget to keep them busy rather than figuring out what it is that is disturbing the child. Gadgets seem like an easier option out and modern day Moms have no qualms in handing an iPad to their child to have him entertain himself with some games or some cartoons. What we don't realize is that gadgets are just a part time solution to resolving any behavioral or habits of your child. Once you give the leverage to your child to demand specifically for a gadget when he is throwing a tantrum, you are asking for trouble. Not only will that spoil your child since he will understand that throwing a tantrum is acceptable since he will get what he demands. Secondly, he will get used to having gadgets around and then there is no separating him from the gadget. As a Supermom in today's world, you need to ensure that you are doing more than just giving in to your child's every whim and fancy and definitely ensuring that whatever you do, your child is not sitting with a gadget 24/7. If at all your child is entrusted with a gadget, make sure that you know what your child is using the gadget for. The last thing you would want as a parent is your child downloading pornography or visiting websites which are not so child-friendly on any of the gadgets given to them.

I know it is difficult to say no to children these days unlike what it was when we were being raised by our Moms. Our mother's never had a problem turning down our requests especially when we were throwing tantrums with a strict 'No' and their no meant for sure we could forget about getting anything we were demanding for. Unlike these days when a mother says 'No' to her child, she gives in to the child's demands after a while since the last thing she wants is to see her child upset. In older days, children always wanted to please their parents; these days however, it seems to be the opposite. As mother's we are so worried about our child being upset with us, we go all out and are willing to do absolutely anything to please them and give in to all their whims and fancies just so that they can go and proclaim about how awesome their Moms are. Let's face it, as a mother, you will always be awesome. You do not have to give in to every demand of your child and that includes giving them your gadgets just so that you can be left in peace. Once a habit catches on, you will find it difficult for your child to give up that habit. Push your children to go out and play or pick up any hobby which does not include them being glued to gadgets.

Due to changes in the modern way of upbringing, children have learned to play by their own rules which means that parents especially mothers have no say in correcting their behavior. Children would prefer to negotiate the rules and punishments doles out to them rather than obey and follow the rules laid down by parents.

When our parents would tell us to go to our rooms as a punishment, we didn't argue with them and had nothing else to do besides staring at the ceiling. Now if you tell your child to go their room, it's less of a punishment and more of a solo party in their room. Once you get your child accustomed to being around gadgets all the time, there is no way any punishment you give your kids is going to benefit them. They will go to their room and in all likelihood post a status on their social media account. As funny as this may sound, it is becoming quite a trend and to avoid being called out publicly, parents now shy away from punishing their children. Discipline is a must for all children, but with changing times, we can expect less of that for sure. There are some things that pass on from generation to generation, things like confidence, courtesy, love and respect. Mothers impart these values to their child and it is values like these which help nurture and shape up your children. Arianna Thomas, a working mother of three residing in the bay area feels that mother's these days are way past the Supermoms of the 80's. She feels some Moms today have the flexibility in what they do and it is on their own terms.

As a parent myself, raising children with the help of gadgets needs to stop. A line needs to be drawn; we need to get back to old school methods which will help in bringing order back to our families. As mothers we deserve the due respect which unfortunately is not given to us anymore in the family. We need to work with our children and partner to ensure our children don't miss out on having a fun childhood rather than sitting at home in their rooms in front of some gadgets gifted to them to perform better at school.

Once you start making small changes and practice them on a daily basis, you will realize that old school ways of being a Supermom always trump being a modern Supermom.

Chapter 15: Discovering Your Own Parenting Personality

So you are about to have a child. Well then, your life is just about to change forever. Bringing a child into the world will most definitely shake your foundation and turn your life upside down. So, as an individual, as a new parent, you need to be stable and have a strong sense of who you are. By knowing your strengths and weaknesses, you will be able to give your best to your child, and minimize the frustration.

Becoming a parent does not mean that you will completely lose yourself, but you will certainly have to change a lot of habits and it might not be as easy as it seems at first. Your child will become the center of your life, especially in the first few years. Babies and toddlers depend on you for every single thing, so in essence, you are an extension of them. They need you to feed them and help them go to the bathroom because they have never done those things before. These are however only the basic needs. You are in for a much longer ride. This is the reason why it is it is important to know who you are so you can better deal with the changes that are about to take over your life.

To keep your sanity intact, you will have to try to squeeze in some time for yourself, even as a new parent. It will be difficult, but you should make every effort to do this. Have your partner watch the child for a few hours a week, so you can go to a spa or to the gym. If you are married or in a relationship, make sure you also go out on dates on a regular basis to renew your adult time. Have a trusted friend or family member babysit for you a few times a month.

You know yourself better than anyone. If you are a very patient person by nature, most likely you will be extra patient with your child. If you are a hyperactive person that needs to constantly be busy, it might be difficult for you in the first year or so of your child's life, as he or she will be mainly sleeping and eating during this time. Recognizing these traits about yourself will help you decide which parent is more suited to stay home with the child, or even if it is a good idea for you to stay home with your child for more than a few months after its birth.

Being a parent means you will never sleep the same again. You will hear every little noise your child makes during the night, and you will have to get used to an irregular sleep schedule at first. Your body might suffer from lack of sleep. So if you are a person who normally needs a lot of sleep, make sure that you nap when the baby naps. If you are someone who dislike mess, you also might have to adjust, because as your toddler starts walking and playing with toys, you will have a daily mess to clean up. Are you a germaphobe? If so, get plenty of sanitizer dispensers around the house, as you will be changing diapers, wiping behinds and cleaning up messes constantly!

Some parents, male or female, are simply a better fit to stay home with the baby, or deal with children of different ages. For example, one parent might be fine talking to the baby all day, while the other one desperately needs adult conversations to retain their sanity.

Get to know yourself, so you can be better prepared for this wonderful and exciting new journey. Read about parenting. Talk to other parents. Most of all, always remember that everything will be ok. You are nervous and that's normal. You are anxious—also normal. No parent becomes a parent totally prepared and ready. You will learn as you go and you will experience the joy of being a parent one day at a time.

Chapter 16: A New Idea: Put Yourself First

Parenting is the hardest job in the world. I doubt anyone would argue with that, but while we put our children's needs high on our agenda, we often fail to take care of the most important person in the parenting equation. Ourselves.

As mothers, we have a natural instinct to place the needs of our children before our own. We tend to their every need, keeping a watchful eye on everything they do to ensure their safety. We nurture them and help them grow, take care of them when they are sick but often this comes at the detriment of our own self-care. While we devote our time to the wellbeing of our family, as mothers we often come way down the list for this kind of love.

Taking care of your own wellbeing is just as important than taking care of your children. If you are unwell, physically or emotionally, who will hold down the fort? How can you begin to take care of others if you don't take proper care of yourself?

When you put your own wellbeing as a priority, you are able to give freely to your children, knowing that because you took care of yourself, you have placed yourself in a position to model self-love and self-esteem which will have huge benefits for your family as a whole.

Good parents should always tend to the needs of their children. No one would suggest that you should neglect the needs of your family, however, it is important to strike a balance. Too much self-sacrifice will work against you.

Neglecting your own health and needs can be damaging to the entire family unit, having negative effects which could continue well into the future, eventually placing your care needs in the hands of your adult children. Taking care of yourself, starting now, will have a positive effect going forward. And although it may seem selfish to put yourself first, try and put that feeling to one side while you read this book and see how putting yourself first will make you are better, happier parent.

Deciding To Make A Change

There's an old saying that "If Mom ain't happy, ain't nobody happy!" In my own family, I've found this saying to be too true! The mother sets the tone for the entire family and it's up to her to bring balance and joy to the home.

This can sound like quite a tall order. Sometimes, I'm feeling anything but joyful or balanced. And yet my children are there, all of the time, looking for that never-ending unconditional love. They are naturally inclined to be simply joyful and when I'm out of sync with that our whole family seems to fall apart.

It is very easy as a mother to neglect one's own self-care. The competing demands of tending to our children, while also juggling the many other roles and responsibilities in our lives and careers, can leave very little time for self-care activities—or inactivities, as the case might be. Self-care and self-nurturing are foundational to our well-being and effectiveness, as mothers and as human beings. We not only have our children to love and care for, and our partners, but also ourselves.

The reality is that we need to invest time in ourselves in order to operate at full efficiency. So often, when we are very busy, we let go of the things that are most rejuvenating and energizing to us in order to do more. We believe we are making the right choices as we are checking more items off our to-do lists, without realising the consequences to our work-life satisfaction, including our sense of productivity at work and our contentment outside of our jobs. We assume that we can become more successful at work by skipping the routine of caring for ourselves, when, in fact, it is often the opposite. Yes, leaving self-care out temporarily may help us in the short term to meet deadlines or increase output, but an absence of self-care in our lives over the long term often has detrimental effects—on our health, emotions, motivation, efficiency, creativity and productivity. One of the most important areas to reconsider is the need for sleep, as it is one of the most neglected and most important areas of self-care for busy mothers. Whether you have a newborn who wakes you up several times a night or active teens who cause you to lose sleep due to worry, there are ways to improve both the quantity and quality of your sleep.

Chapter 17: Raising Strong-Willed And Self-Confident Children

While all these principles are great, sometimes, it can be quite challenging to deal with a strong willed child who knows what they want and how they want it. So, how do you deal with strong willed children? How do you ensure that you don't break their will and thus affect their self-esteem? How do you ensure that you raise children who are confident in their abilities? Many parents can identify with these questions. We will thus look at how best to parent a strong-willed child and how to ensure that you bring up self-confident children.

How to Parent a Strong-Willed Child

While strong-willed children can be a challenge to raise when young, if raised well, they turn out to be responsible and self-motivated teens and finally adults. They are the kind of children who will not easily succumb to peer pressure and will always be go-getters. Such children are likely to be disciplined, know what they want to achieve and how to get it. They are also likely to be more confident. So the challenge is, how do you raise such children to have all these great qualities?

Use Routines and Rules to Avoid Power Struggles

This is important as they will know that your household has a particular schedule that everyone has to follow and instead of feeling as though you are bossing them, they will simply know that there is a simple schedule that not only them but everyone has to adhere to. This is why it is important that you are careful how you act since failure for you to follow the schedule will bring great problems.

Always Know that Strong-Willed Children Learn Through Experimenting

This means that before they can or cannot do anything, they must see for themselves. They would for instance want to know that the stove is hot so unless you are worried about injury, the only way that they can learn is through experience rather than trying to control them. Such a child will also want to test your limits until they learn and once they do, they adapt and move on.

Your Strong-Willed Child Desires Mastery

Allow your child to take charge of their activities. Allow them to select the activities they are supposed to do every morning, for instance. When your child feels like they are more independent and in charge, they are unlikely to show opposition.

Allow your Strong-Willed Child to Choose From Several Choices

Rather than bark orders, why not offer them choices. This is important as it makes your child feel like they are in charge. If for instance you have an appointment that they have to attend and they want to play, you can ask, "Do you want to leave now or in 15 minutes?" If it is 15 minutes then agree on that and allow them to play for 15 minutes then remind them to keep their word.

Don't Push your Child into Opposing you

Having a hard position can easily make your child defy you. Remember we talked about the importance of flexibility in parenting. Try to be flexible but also consistent. Rather than focus on winning an argument and showing your child who has the authority, why not concentrate on what's important, which is the relationship you have with your child.

Learn to Listen to your Child

In most cases, as adults, we assume that we know best; hence, it is very easy for us not to want to listen to our children. However, remember that your strong willed child will hold onto their views unless you reassure them otherwise. For instance, your son may not want to take a bath because they are afraid they will go down the drain like the water. While this may seem trivial to you, it is something huge for them. Rather than tell them that they are being silly, how about installing a suitable drain stopper and you can have your child put it every time they are taking a shower so that they don't go down the drain. Such simple things will make your child feel loved.

See it from their Point of View

If for instance, you break a promise and your child gets mad because you did, try and apologize to them rather than think that they are being stubborn. Remember your child will be thinking why it is okay for you to break a promise and they cannot break their promise to you. Remember what we said about leading by example.

How to Raise Confident Children

While raising a strong-willed child is a great challenge for many parents, raising a self-confident child is equally challenging. We will look at ways you can bring up self-confident children.

Learn to Accept your Child

You need to understand that every child is different. Some kids love their space while others love to be the center of attention. If your child prefers to only have one friend then don't take this to mean that they are unsocial; they may just feel close to that one person and are not interested in making another friend. You should also not try to compare your social skills with your child. I have heard many parents say how they have many friends but their child does not even have a friend. Rather than try to force your child to make friends, why not find out why they don't want to have friends. They may just be shy and need some help or they may just love their space. Therefore, avoid comparing as this can make your child feel unaccepted and this would definitely affect her self-esteem.

Rather than Praise, Encourage

While you may think that praising your child for an achievement is great, it may turn out not to be such a great idea after all. Praising your child means that you are only evaluating her on the end product rather than the effort they put in. Your child may thus be so afraid of not getting that 'A' again. If your child puts so much effort into getting that nice grade and they are unable to achieve that goal, this can affect their self-confidence as they will immediately think that they are failures. Therefore, emphasize on the effort put and improvement to show your child that you are noticing every progress they are making.

Stop being a Control Freak and Start to Coach

Coaches are amazing as they help the child develop the specific skills to play a game for instance. Your job as your parent is to ensure that your child flourishes and this means taking the time to identify their skills rather than trying to control them. As a coach, you will know their strengths and weaknesses and thus focus on helping them on working on their weaknesses to improve and become better individuals.

Remember that No One is Perfect

It is so amazing how parents think that it is okay for them to make mistakes but not their children. Children are human beings bound to make mistakes like any one. Trying to make your child feel so bad because they have not achieved a certain goal can wound their self-esteem. It is so sad when you see a child trying so hard to please the father who does not think that what their child has done is good enough.

Give Age Appropriate Tasks

While your teen child can help with the dishes, your younger child may not be able to do so but they can help you sort out laundry. Giving a child age appropriate tasks makes the child have an easier time doing the task and they are likely to do it well. However, if you give a child a difficult task and are unable to do it well, they feel bad about themselves that they were unable to do something. Therefore, to avoid such problems it is best to give tasks that are suitable for a particular age.

Encourage Positive Self-Talk

Did you know that something as simple as positive self-talk can improve our ability to do a difficult task? Telling your child how an idiot they are or how incompetent they are only discourages them and for sure your child will not try again. Therefore, even when your child seems not to be getting something, encourage them rather than call them names. You can even stop undertaking the task altogether and look at it later when everyone is fresh and not tired.

Chapter 18: Question Of Financial Security

Mothers are always the **multitasking-machine** of every household. They manage a lot of work starting from the kids homework, keeping a check on their report card, adjusting to their various other demands, their play dates, their food, their health and numerous other activities.

However, the situation definitely becomes difficult when it is only the mother who has to look after the kids. She has to manage the finances along with the household, without letting the kid feel deprived.

When you are a single mother, you are the sole breadwinner of the family. Your kid will look up to you for all his/her needs.

Managing the finances along with trying to give the kid a living a decent life can sometimes be very challenging for a single mom. Following are some of the ideas on how a single mom can maintain a **financial security** for managing herself and her kid/s.

Invest Wisely and Know the Right Time for the Right Choice:

Being a single mother, you have to maintain a **strict budget** and accounts for all kinds of expenses. If you are used to taking monthly pedicures or go for some mindless shopping trips every once in a while, now is the time to cut down every tiny bit of it.

Go through the finances and make a right budget according to the situation. That is the first step every single mother has to take to maintain financial stability. Being in a financial mess is definitely a bad space to be in, especially when you are a single mother. Therefore, you need to make it a point to save as much and wherever you can.

Differentiating between what **your needs and what your wants** are, is the first step in managing your finances. For example, for books, music and movies you can always head towards the library. Other expenses like buying a car or the big house are always important, but at the same time getting the kids admitted into one of the good schools is more important. You have to decide and make the right choices, based on the importance and the urgency of the matter.

Saving for the Future:

As a single mother, you need to keep in mind the various expenses that your child may incur in the future, mainly his or her tuition fees, **college education** or health insurance.

As a mother, you need to get **health insurance** for yourself too. Remember, you are the only one that your child looks up to. You are also the only one who is responsible for your child. Under such a condition, if anything happens to you, your child needs the financial security and a well-insured future.

However, while investing in insurances, you need to be well aware of the various rates, interests and other small details that matter big time.

Having an emergency savings fund too greatly helps.

Interacting with Other People and with the Child:

Talking with other people (**single parents**) going through similar experiences helps a lot, in sorting out some of the problems that you may be going through. For this you can join various **social groups** or online forums. These groups may also help you in making a close-knit group of friends, who are always there to help each other during distress. For example, if you can't afford a babysitter, then you can always seek help from one of these friends.

Another important thing is to talk to your child frankly about the **financial situation**. Make your kid understand the fact that it is difficult being a single mom and managing all expenses by yourself. Your child needs to be aware of the financial situation that you are in, due to lack of one parent. This way your child will understand the value of money and will also be encouraged to be independent at an early age.

Chapter 19: Tips For Raising An Emotional Child

Generally, parents tend to ignore their child's emotions since they try to pay attention to the behaviors and not feelings. By knowing your child's psychological condition, you'll be more attuned to our children and learn methods to raise an emotionally healthy child. Here are some of the parenting principles to help you.

· Never ignore signs that your child is having problems.

Make sure you know the behavioral changes that can indicate a child is suffering. If a teacher opens up that your child has issues interacting with other children in a class, don't take it merely as a bad habit while hoping for the best. What might begin as a small habit pattern can extend into later habits that are more severe. For example, an extreme concentration on video games or food could denote symptoms that a child is using those things to reduce pain. If not handled swiftly, these patterns might lead to drug and alcohol addiction or obesity.

· Avoid trivializing how your child is feeling.

It isn't easy for most parents to cope with their children's moods, so they often attribute them to growth stages such as the terrible twos or teen rebellion. While those stages contribute to emotional behavior, it's imperative to understand to relate to your child when they're in that state and teach them ways to handle their emotions.

Once you realize an emotional shift in your child, make sure you discover what's affecting them and act accordingly. Maybe they are scared of something that doesn't make sense, or they're ready to talk about it? When your child understands that you're concerned about their struggles, you try to help them scrutinize their emotions to understand the sources better. You need to be nonjudgmental and open to encourage the child to be truthful with you. Providing the two responses will help establish a constructive attitude that your child will also adopt. This will help the child develop a resiliency that will serve well in upcoming struggles.

- Be sensitive and attuned and not reactive.

From the time they start speaking first words, it's imperative to motivate children to talk to you. When you want to influence your child, making rules won't work, but maintaining an equal and open sense of communication will excel. But for this to work, you need to be responsible. Make sure you live your words for your child to trust you. In case you invite your child to talk to you honestly, but you seem erratic or defensive in your response, then you give them a good reason not to open up regarding what she's enduring.

As a parent, you need to make sure you don't act defensively to your children You must apologize that their emotions were affected and assist them in making sense of their specific potential and experience. After that, you can share your feelings about their actions as you both enjoy the same honest level of communication. If you slip away and act in an inappropriate and insensitive way, you can repair the damage to your child's trust with an opportunity to communicate with you.

· Invite the child to spend some time with you.

When you want to spend time with your child, quality is more essential than quantity. It's recommended you set a unique time where you can engage in things directed by your child. A realistic duration where you provide your child with uninterrupted attention and allow them to know they're your top priority. Allowing your child to decide what you do doesn't imply you enable them to set unrealistic goals about tasks that will cost a lot of money and time. You're just offering a chance to share a task with your child and develop a situation where they will talk to you.

You'll have a chance to learn about the child from what they say you do or the type of games to play. Parents who spare some time to spend with their children as they play with toys or action figures are always surprised to hear their child saying the same things that their mother expresses or acting in ways that their dad does.

· If the child doesn't talk to you, assist them in formulating shared trust.

The majority of parents don't know what to do whenever their children fail to open up. While your child declines your offerings, it's essential to keep reminding them that you're there for them when they want to open up. Make sure you're always there for the child since you don't know when they might come around.

If the child doesn't feel comfortable opening up to you, bear in mind that it's not bad to help one find a person she can trust and talk to. Everyone has that one person who was a mentor to him or her as children. Allowing your child to know it's okay to open up to someone apart from you will help establish trust and motivate her to deal with one's emotions.

- Get them the required help when in real trouble.

If a child expresses an abnormal amount of anxiety, anger, stress, pain, or fear, it's imperative to get them the required help. As a parent, you don't have to be extremely prideful when raising your child. The way your child feels must outweigh how you're viewed as her parent. The greatest thing you can do for her is to be selfless in your devotion to giving her emotional help.

- Check your emotional health.

Even though it's vital to prioritize the needs of your child, it's equally pivotal to remember that little impacts your child more than how you're feeling. Naturally, children are attuned to the moods of their parents. Wearing a brave smile or repudiating your frustrations cannot mask what you are feeling. Your child will perceive those feelings and affect her equally.

So, making sure you take care of your mental wellbeing is a mandatory factor in assisting your child in feeling happy. Irrespective of how you fuss over, pay attention to her or worry about her, you need to feel contented and fulfilled in yourself.

How to grow and be a more effective parent.

Raising children is tough but a fulfilling task. Here are some child-raising tips to help you feel like an accomplished parent:

I. Boost Your Child's Self-Esteem.

Children begin having their sense of self as toddlers once they see themselves in the eyes of their parents. The children absorb your body language, tone of voice, and all your expressions. Your actions and words play a vital role in their growth as they'll develop their self-esteem.

Applauding achievements, irrespective of how small it might be, will make the children feel proud. Allowing them to do various activities on their own will make them feel strong and responsible. In contrast, demeaning comments and comparing a child unfavorably with others will make her feel unworthy.

Don't make full statements or use your words as weapons. Remarks such as "What a silly thing to do!" or "You're acting more like a baby than your sister!" will cause more damage. So, pick your words carefully and make sure you are compassionate. Let your child understand that every person makes mistakes, and you still love them, even when you dislike their habits.

II. Catch the child doing good things.

Have you tried to think about the number of times you've reacted negatively to your child in a single day? You might realize that you criticize more than complementing. How would you feel if you were treated with too much negativity?

The most effective method is to get your children doing something encouraging. For instance, you can tell them, "Wow, you cleaned your room without being asked-, that's awesome!" or "I was watching as you play with your brother, and you were patient." These remarks will encourage good habits for a long time than frequent scolding.

Try to find something positive to praise your child and make sure you're generous by rewarding her with hugs and lots of love. This will help nurture good behaviors.

III. Create limits while being steady with your discipline.

Discipline is essential is every family. The objective of discipline is to assist children in selecting acceptable habits and learning self-control. They might test the limits you develop for them, but the restrictions will help them grow into responsible people.

Creating house regulations assists children to know your expectations and have self-control. These rules include no watching TV until they complete homework, not using abusive language, no hitting, or hurtful teasing.

You may need to put a system in your home, such as a warning, followed by punishments such as loss of privileges like playing video games. The majority of parents fail to comply with the punishments, and this is a huge mistake. You cannot discipline your child for talking back the first day and then overlook it the following day. Try to be consistent as it'll teach them what to expect.

IV. Create time for your children.

It's always hard for parents and children to come together during a family meal, left alone spending time together. So, wake up ten minutes earlier in the morning to eat breakfast with them or take a walk after eating dinner. Children who don't get the attention they need from their caregivers act out or misbehave around since they know they'll be noticed that way.

The majority of parents find it beneficial to set some time and spend with their children. Make a special night every week to be with the child and let them decide ways to spend the time. Find ways to connect, such as putting a note or something nice in your child's lunchbox.

Never should you feel guilty if you're a working parent. It's the little things you will do, such as playing cards, making popcorn, and window shopping that your child will remember.

V. Be the role model.

Children tend to learn a lot about the way to react through imitating their parents. The younger the child, the more he or she is taking cues from you. Before lashing out and blowing your top in the presence of your child, ask yourself: Is that the way you want the child to act when they're irritated? Note that your children are watching you. Research indicates that children who hit others always have role models for violence back at home.

Have the traits you want to see in your children: respect, honesty, friendliness, tolerance, and kindness. Display unselfish behavior every time. Help other people without expecting anything in return. Show gratitude and give compliments. Most importantly, treat your children the way you want other individuals to treat you.

VI. Communication should be your priority

Never expect your children to do everything just because you said so. They need and deserve explanations like adults. If you fail to explain, they'll start wondering about your values and intentions, and if they have any basis. Reasoning with your children gives them a chance to learn and understand things in a nonjudgmental manner.

Your expectations should be clear; and if there's an issue, explain it, express what you feel, and allow your child to work on the remedy with you. Remember to include punishments. Give suggestions as you provide choice and make sure you are open to her ideas. Discuss to collaboratively find the best recommendation. Children who take part in the decision-making process tend to be more motivated to perform the tasks.

VII. Be flexible and ready to adjust your parenting method.

If you always feel disappointed by your child's behavior, maybe you have unrealistic expectations? A kid's environment has a considerable impact on one's actions, so you can try to change the environment to change the behavior. If you realize you continue saying no to your child who's 2, find ways to change your surroundings such that fewer things will be off-limits. That will reduce frustration for you and your baby.

As the child changes, you'll need to adjust your parenting method. What might work with your child now might not work in one or two years to come.

Teenagers tend to look to their peers for role models than their parents. Despite that, don't stop offering guidance, encouragement, and proper discipline as you allow the teenager to get more confidence.

VIII. Give your child unconditional love.

Since you're the parent, you are accountable for guiding and correcting your child. However, the way you express your counteractive guidance will create a difference in the ways the child will receive it.

If you must confront your child, don't blame, criticize, or fault-find, as these things will damage self-esteem and result in bitterness. Instead, try to encourage and nurture, even when it comes to disciplining the child. Ensure that she understands that although you expect and want better from her next time, you still love her irrespective of the situation.

Chapter 20: Begin The Approach Early

Babies are adorable and cuddly during the earliest stages of life and require only being fed when he/she is hungry or have a clean change when needed. Newborns need to feel secure and safe since they have been totally sheltered for nine months.

Infants do begin learning early concerning some of the constraints in life such as feeding schedules and dependency on the parents for necessary attention upon demand. Taking care of your child's needs will help him/her become independent later in life. Beyond that, until the child becomes a toddler the time is not considered a time of disciplinary actions.

Children have a curious nature and love to explore every element in the new space provided outside of the crib or playpen.

The program for discipline needs a bit of adjustment for the parent's sanity as well as the safety of the toddler. Infants respond to the nurturing parent and will also expect guidance if he/she is in danger.

Some days your schedule has more cuddling time than others. It is important to spend quality time with your child so confidence and self-esteem can become a part of his or her life. The quality time spent with your youngster can change negative attitudes into a full blown happy child.

The Transitional Time

Loving parents realize mistakes will happen whether it is from the child or the parent's viewpoint. Children don't come equipped with instruction manuals, and each child is uniquely different. As the baby grows from infancy into the toddler stage (from ages one until three), you will realize it is time to begin to set what limits are necessary and make the boundaries apparent with love and kindness.

Discipline is practiced each time you escort your child out of a dangerous situation. The early stages begin with simply removing the distraction. Placing objects such as a tempting treat on the table or a hot drink away from the toddler's reach is also a form of training and discipline. The training can be done in a loving way so the child understands the danger and can associate a slight rise in the voice as a signal of distress.

Four to Seven Month Discipline Scenario

As your baby approaches early development during the four to seven-month time frame, you will begin to notice the differences between what your baby needs and want he/she wants. For beginners, it isn't essential to hold your bundle of joy until sleepy time. Babies need to learn to fall asleep without your assistance.

Exploration begins when babies learn how to grasp everything with the discovery of hand movements. Hair and jewelry are good places to start the adventure. You can't respond by reacting negatively, so you should simply put the baby down, and remove the distraction. This action is one of the steps which will set the platform for discipline at a later time.

Teething is another episode of development which can begin at any time after three months, but some babies will wait until around six months old. If you are breastfeeding, you baby might give you an extra hard nibble/bite. Some mothers will merely push the baby's nose close to her body until the baby releases. This will promptly let the baby know; NO biting is allowed.

Seven to Twelve Months Discipline Scenario

The time has come to cover light sockets, install baby gates, install child-resistant cabinet locks, and remove any dangerous or poisonous items out of your infant's reach. Providing a safe environment is your job and with these obstacles removed, you will provide the NO you are searching for without the drama of bellowing at your child for the new challenges.

Try leaving one cabinet in your kitchen without a lock. You can choose to place some items in the cabinet that will provide entertainment for your crawler. Place plastic utensils and plates or other toys in the cabinet to mimic the items you use in your kitchen every day. Your baby will enjoy creating a new imaginative dish just for you. The bonus will mean you don't have to provide any discipline for a happy toddler.

If you're noticing your baby has become clingier, it may well be signs of separation anxiety which is traditional with many babies. You can train your kid to create playtime exploitation using his/her imagination for entertainment.

If you are doing household chores and the baby begins to cry after you leave the space, don't rush back. Merely, say it is okay using a calm voice. This action is also teaching a form of discipline.

Twelve to Eighteen Months Discipline Scenario

During this six month span, your child will begin to exercise his/her vocal cords in an attempt to strengthen them. You have to teach your child when it is appropriate behavior to make the new screeching noises. Suggest going outside in the yard for the release.

The quiet voice method needs to be practiced before you are in a jam-packed restaurant or worse yet, in a church or library. It is an excellent idea to bring favorite 'quiet' items with you for special outings. If the noise becomes out of control, it is essential to remove your child from the area.

Self-control has not yet been learned, and the child hasn't learned to distinguish what is acceptable. He or she might have been enjoying the scenery, but discipline was shown when the child was removed.

Eighteen to Twenty-four Months Discipline Scenario

Rebellion and self-sufficiency are huge issues during this phase of child development. Children can become frustrated because you don't yet understand exactly what he/she wants. The process of elimination begins. Your child is clueless concerning the dangers involved with his/her curiosity since mobility is now raging. He or she is fearless and impulsive without realizing it is a recipe for disaster and—yes—discipline.

If the child is overreacting because a toy is out of reach, try to express his or her feelings. You could say, "Would you like me to get your toy for you? I can reach it." This response will eliminate the issue without making a spectacle. The positive approach is the best tool you possess.

Frustration can produce biting and hitting other children or pets during this developmental phase. Once again, remove the child from the situation, and let him/her know it is unacceptable because biting hurts. These two movements can be signs of underlying issues. Ask yourself if the child is doing this during similar events or at the same time of the day. Discover any trigger points that could cause the actions.

Distraction is an excellent choice of discipline for a rebellious child. If your youngster doesn't want to brush his/her hair, make it a song game. Your child will associate the fun with a chore that is normally disliked. After all, children love challenging games.

Conclusion

Thank you again for downloading this book!

I hope that this book was able to help you to understand the transition that takes place during the teenage years and prepare you for it. Hopefully, we can all come out being successful parents with well-adjusted teenagers.

The next step is to spend time with your teenagers and just have a wonderful life together, without the drama.

Thank you and good luck!

www.ingramcontent.com/pod-product-compliance
Lightning Source LLC
Chambersburg PA
CBHW072012070526
44583CB00015B/1454